NATIVE AMERICAN NATIONS

THE NEZ PERCE

BY BETTY MARCKS

CONSULTANT: TIM TOPPER, CHEYENNE RIVER SIOUX

BLASTOFF! DISCOVERY

BELLWETHER MEDIA • MINNEAPOLIS, MN

Author's Statement of Positionality:
I am a white woman of European descent. As such, I can claim no direct lived experience of being a Native American. In writing this book, however, I have tried to be an ally by relying on sources by Native American writers and authors whenever possible and have worked to let their voices guide its content.

This edition first published in 2025 by Bellwether Media, Inc.

No part of this publication may be reproduced in whole or in part without written permission of the publisher. For information regarding permission, write to Bellwether Media, Inc.,
Attention: Permissions Department,
6012 Blue Circle Drive, Minnetonka, MN 55343.

Library of Congress Cataloging-in-Publication Data

Names: Marcks, Betty, author.
Title: The Nez Perce / by Betty Marcks.
Description: Minneapolis, MN : Bellwether Media, Inc., 2025. | Series: Blastoff! discovery: Native American nations | Includes bibliographical references and index. | Audience: Ages 7-12 | Audience: Grades 4-6 | Summary: "Engaging images accompany information about the Nez Perce. The combination of high-interest subject matter and narrative text is intended for students in grades 3 through 8" – Provided by publisher.
Identifiers: LCCN 2024016017 (print) | LCCN 2024016018 (ebook) | ISBN 9798893040081 (library binding) | ISBN 9798893041507 (paperback) | ISBN 9781644879405 (ebook)
Subjects: LCSH: Nez Percé Indians–Juvenile literature.
Classification: LCC E99.N5 M18 2025 (print) | LCC E99.N5 (ebook) | DDC 979.5004/974124–dc23/eng/20240513
LC record available at https://lccn.loc.gov/2024016017
LC ebook record available at https://lccn.loc.gov/2024016018

Text copyright © 2025 by Bellwether Media, Inc. BLASTOFF! DISCOVERY and associated logos are trademarks and/or registered trademarks of Bellwether Media, Inc. Bellwether Media is a division of Chrysalis Education Group.

Editor: Elizabeth Neuenfeldt   Series Designer: Andrea Schneider
Book Designer: Laura Sowers

Printed in the United States of America, North Mankato, MN.

TABLE OF CONTENTS

THE PEOPLE	4
TRADITIONAL NEZ PERCE LIFE	6
EUROPEAN CONTACT	12
LIFE TODAY	16
CONTINUING TRADITIONS	20
FIGHT TODAY, BRIGHT TOMORROW	24
TIMELINE	28
GLOSSARY	30
TO LEARN MORE	31
INDEX	32

ENTERING NEZ PERCE INDIAN RESERVATION

THE PEOPLE

The Nez Perce are a nation of Native American peoples. They call themselves *Nimiipuu*, or "The People." Their original lands cover areas of today's Idaho, Oregon, and Washington. Their land spans valleys, **prairies**, mountains, **plateaus**, and vast rivers.

The Nez Perce believe their people have called their lands home forever. The Nez Perce creation story tells of a monster that began eating the animals. Coyote killed the monster and helped the animals escape. Coyote scattered pieces of the monster throughout the land. The pieces became the different tribes.

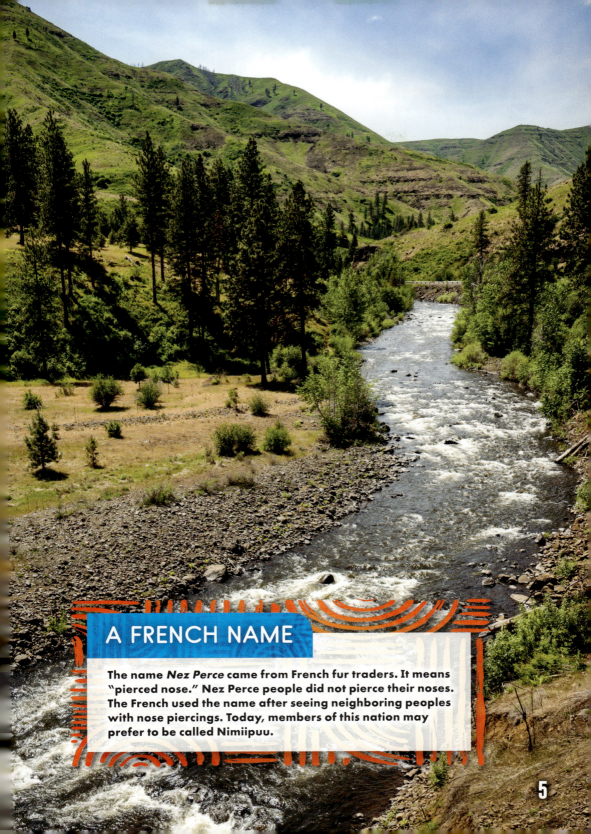

A FRENCH NAME

The name *Nez Perce* came from French fur traders. It means "pierced nose." Nez Perce people did not pierce their noses. The French used the name after seeing neighboring peoples with nose piercings. Today, members of this nation may prefer to be called Nimiipuu.

TRADITIONAL NEZ PERCE LIFE

Ancestral Nez Perce mostly lived in independent villages built along rivers, especially in winter. Each village was led by a Chief or Headman. This person was chosen by a **council** of Elders. Neighboring villages were organized into **bands**. They had close ties to one another.

Men and women carried out different roles within each village. Men hunted, fished, and engaged in war. They also made the tools they needed to complete these duties. Women cared for their homes and children. They gathered and prepared food. They also made household tools such as baskets.

SOCKEYE SALMON

FISH TRAP

Ancestral Nez Perce relied on the **natural resources** around them. Fish was a **staple** food. Men often caught fish with nets that were weighed down with stones called sinkers. They mostly caught salmon and trout. They hunted large game including elk, moose, bighorn sheep, and deer. They also hunted birds and beavers.

Women gathered plants such as wild carrots, eggs, and berries. They carried foods and other goods in beautifully decorated bags. Weavers would mark their bags with a flaw. This practice showed that only the Creator made perfect things. The bags were special and often passed from one **generation** to the next.

NEZ PERCE TOOLS

HEMP

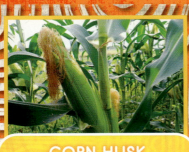

CORN HUSK

NEZ PERCE BAG

Ancestral Nez Perce were introduced to horses by the early 1700s. Horses soon became an important part of their **culture**. Horses made hunting and gathering foods much easier. Hunting groups could travel farther to hunt different animals, such as bison. The people could develop trade relationships and become successful warriors.

APPALOOSA HORSE

Ancestral Nez Perce created the famous **Appaloosa** horses. These horses have spotted coats. They also have striped hooves. They are smart animals. They are bred to travel long distances. The people had huge herds of Appaloosa horses. They were sources of wealth and honor.

EUROPEAN CONTACT

The Nez Perce met members of the Lewis and Clark **expedition** in 1805. They welcomed the white travelers and gave them supplies. They also welcomed white traders and **missionaries** in the years that followed. But white people took Nez Perce lands.

The United States government created the first Nez Perce **reservation** in 1855. White people illegally found gold on the reservation soon after. The U.S. made their reservation lands even smaller. However, many Nez Perce lived outside the reservation. They were ordered to move onto the reservation in 1877.

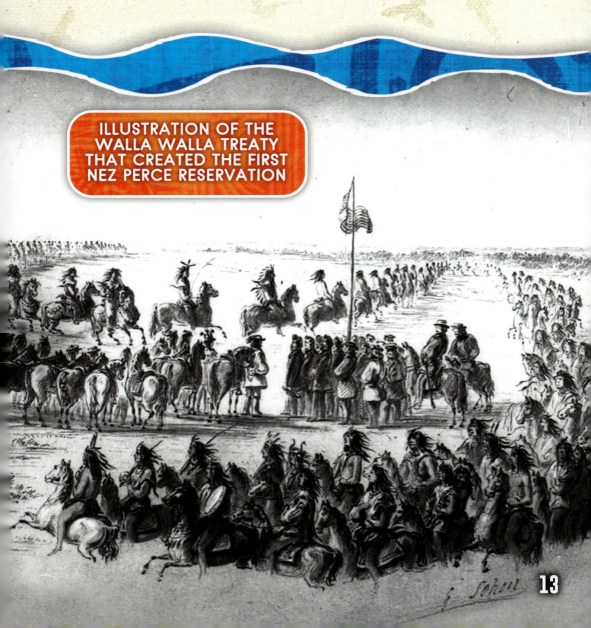

ILLUSTRATION OF THE WALLA WALLA TREATY THAT CREATED THE FIRST NEZ PERCE RESERVATION

Chief Joseph prepared his people to move onto the reservation. But a few Nez Perce warriors attacked a group of **settlers**. They were angry with what was happening to their people. Chief Joseph knew the attack would lead to war. He led his people toward Canada to escape the U.S. Army.

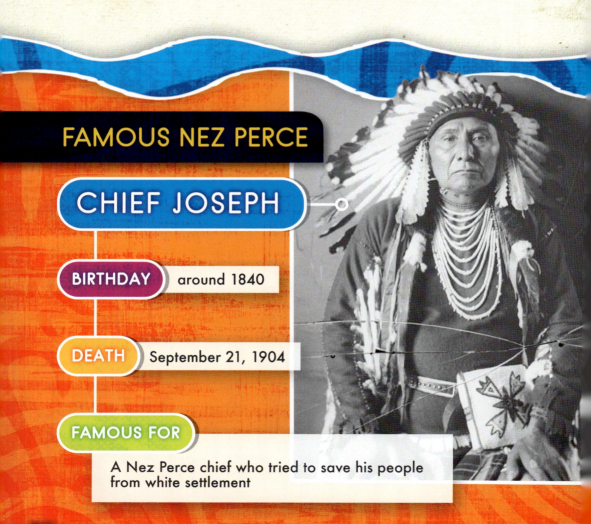

FAMOUS NEZ PERCE

CHIEF JOSEPH

BIRTHDAY around 1840

DEATH September 21, 1904

FAMOUS FOR A Nez Perce chief who tried to save his people from white settlement

CHIEF JOSEPH'S BAND IN 1877

Chief Joseph and his people traveled over 1,000 miles (1,609 kilometers). His warriors were able to defeat the Army in several battles. But they were eventually surrounded just 40 miles (64 kilometers) from Canada. His band was sent to Oklahoma. Many people did not survive. His people were allowed to return to the northwest in 1885.

LIFE TODAY

Today, the Nez Perce nation is made up of more than 3,500 members. Many members of the nation live on the reservation. But people who identify as Nez Perce live throughout the U.S. and the world.

The nation's reservation spans 1,203 square miles (3,116 square kilometers) of western Idaho. This land is a small part of the nation's original land. The Nez Perce nation's government is based in the city of Lapwai, Idaho.

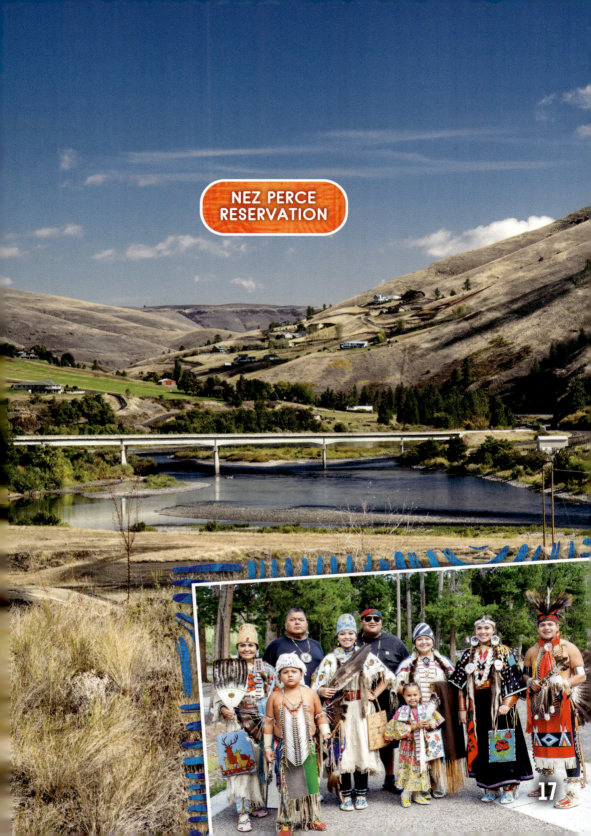

The Nez Perce nation is a federally recognized tribal nation. Its independent government works for the people of the nation. The nine-person Tribal Executive Committee is the leading government body. They make important decisions for the nation. The General Council includes all citizens over the age of 18. They meet twice each year to review the work of the Tribal Executive Committee.

The tribal government provides important services to ensure the health of members and the land. The Tribal Court and police department work to keep the community safe.

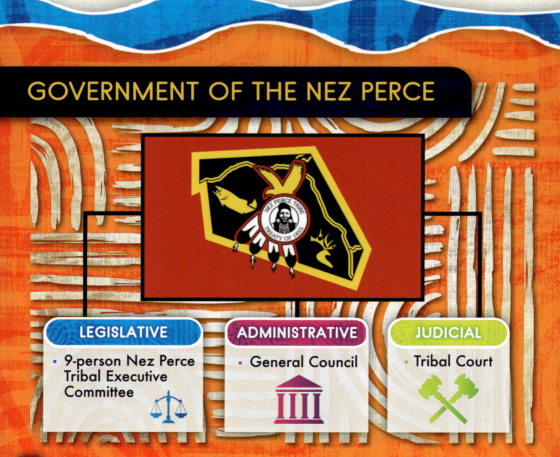

GOVERNMENT OF THE NEZ PERCE

LEGISLATIVE
- 9-person Nez Perce Tribal Executive Committee

ADMINISTRATIVE
- General Council

JUDICIAL
- Tribal Court

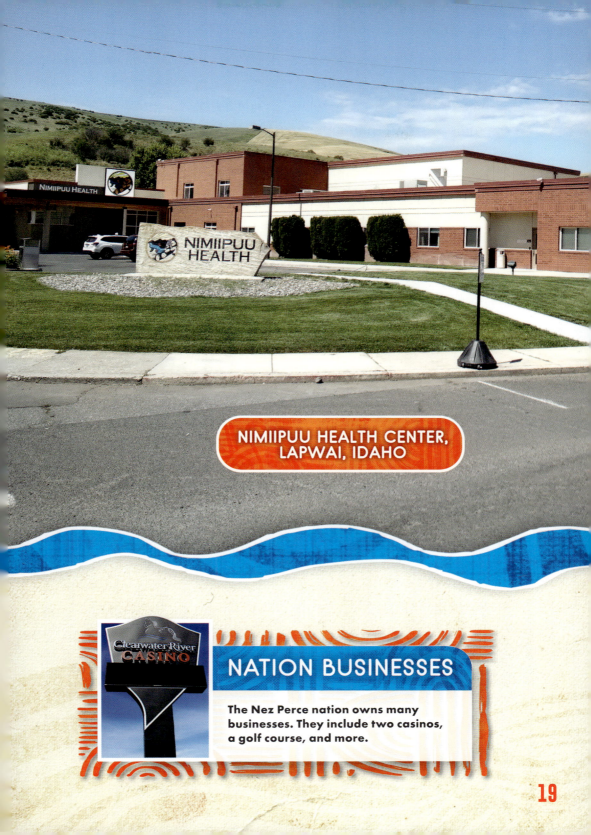

NIMIIPUU HEALTH CENTER, LAPWAI, IDAHO

NATION BUSINESSES

The Nez Perce nation owns many businesses. They include two casinos, a golf course, and more.

CONTINUING TRADITIONS

NEZ PERCE LANGUAGE PROGRAM WEBSITE

Language is a key part of culture. The Nez Perce Language Program helps people learn *nimipuutímt*. It holds in-person classes at the nation's community center. The program's website has lesson plans that teach the language. The lesson plans include **traditional** information through storytelling. They are used at several schools.

The written form of nimipuutímt does not use capital letters. The language has several sounds that are not used when speaking English. There are also some English sounds that are not included in nimipuutímt. The letters b, d, f, g, j, r, v, and z are not used.

RIDERS ON THE NATIONAL CHIEF JOSEPH TRAIL RIDE

The Chief Joseph Foundation hosts the National Chief Joseph Trail Ride each year. Riders on horseback follow the trail their ancestors took to escape the U.S. Army. The trail is 1,300 miles (2,092 kilometers) long. Each year's riders spend five days riding 100 miles (161 kilometers). It takes 13 years to complete the trail. Each year, four or five young riders are chosen to participate alongside other riders.

The ride keeps Nez Perce connected to their **heritage**. Some Nez Perce gather with their Appaloosas to honor their ancestors. They wear clothing that has been passed down from family members.

FRIENDSHIP FEAST

The Nez Perce Friendship Feast takes place each year in late July. It is part of the Chief Joseph Days Rodeo. It is an opportunity for people to build friendships and enjoy traditional foods.

NATIONAL CHIEF JOSEPH TRAIL RIDE MAP

FIGHT TODAY, BRIGHT TOMORROW

SALMON RIVER

The Nez Perce work to keep the land and people safe. The Idaho state government gave an air quality permit to a mining company in 2022. The company wants to mine an area of the Salmon River. The mine would release dangerous chemicals into the air. The permit goes against federal and state laws. It would affect tribal members' rights to fishing and hunting in the area. It would also harm **sacred** sites.

The Nez Perce won a case in 2023. The mining company pays for the nation's water quality improvement program. The Nez Perce will continue to fight to keep the area safe from mining.

25

Fishing is a traditional practice for many Nez Perce. The nation ensures this tradition can carry on by taking care of the rivers throughout their ancestral land. The tribe has a fish program that sets fishing seasons.

The Nez Perce government has many other programs to protect the land and people. One is the Cultural Resources Program. It helps protect **treaty** rights. The Land Services Program makes sure the land is being used responsibly. Each of these programs ensures the land will be protected for the future!

A NEZ PERCE CHAIR MEMBER AND A U.S. GOVERNMENT OFFICIAL WORKING TO PROTECT FISH IN THE COLUMBIA RIVER SYSTEM

A MEMBER OF THE NEZ PERCE DEPARTMENT OF FISHERIES RESOURCES MANAGEMENT WITH A LAMPREY

MANAGING RIVERS

The Department of Fisheries Resources Management is run by the Nez Perce. It employs nearly 200 people. It has over $20 million to use each year to protect waterways in Idaho, Oregon, and Washington.

TIMELINE

LATE 1600s TO EARLY 1700s
The Nez Perce are introduced to horses

1863
The U.S. government forces the Nez Perce to sign a treaty that greatly reduces the size of Nez Perce lands

1885
Nez Perce bands who were forced to move to Oklahoma are allowed to return to the northwest

1855
A treaty with the U.S. government establishes the boundaries of the first Nez Perce reservation

1877
Many Nez Perce are forced to leave their ancestral lands and are followed by the U.S. military for months before they are forced to surrender

1986

The Nez Perce National Historic Trail is established

1997

The Advisory Board of Elders approves a spelling system for nimipuutímt

2020

The Nez Perce nation purchases 0.2 square miles (0.6 square kilometers) of their ancestral land in Oregon

1934

Archie Phinney's *Nez Perce Texts* is released as an important collection of Nez Perce stories

GLOSSARY

ancestral—related to relatives who lived long ago

Appaloosa—a horse breed developed by the Nez Perce that usually has a white or solid-colored coat with small dark spots

bands—groups of people who live as communities and share a culture

council—a group of people who meet to run a government

culture—the beliefs, arts, and ways of life in a place or society

expedition—a journey taken for a specific reason, such as to explore a region

generation—a group of people who were born around the same time

heritage—the traditions, achievements, and beliefs that are part of the history of a group of people

missionaries—people sent to a place to spread a religious faith

natural resources—materials that are found in nature and used by humans

plateaus—areas of flat, raised land

prairies—large, open areas of grassland

reservation—land set aside by the U.S. government for the forced removal of a Native American community from their original land

sacred—relating to spiritual or religious practice

settlers—people who move to live in a new region

staple—a widely used food or other item

traditional—related to customs, ideas, or beliefs handed down from one generation to the next

treaty—related to an official agreement between two groups

TO LEARN MORE

AT THE LIBRARY

Grack, Rachel. *Appaloosa Horses*. Minneapolis, Minn.: Bellwether Media, 2021.

Marcks, Betty. *The Sioux*. Minneapolis, Minn.: Bellwether Media, 2024.

Rathburn, Betsy. *Idaho*. Minneapolis, Minn.: Bellwether Media, 2022.

ON THE WEB

FACTSURFER

Factsurfer.com gives you a safe, fun way to find more information.

1. Go to www.factsurfer.com.

2. Enter "the Nez Perce" into the search box and click 🔍.

3. Select your book cover to see a list of related content.

INDEX

bands, 6, 15
businesses, 19
Chief, 6, 14, 15
Chief Joseph, 14, 15, 22, 23
council, 6, 18
Cultural Resources Program, 26
culture, 4, 6, 7, 8, 9, 10, 11, 20, 21
Department of Fisheries Resources Management, 27
foods, 7, 8, 9, 10, 23
future, 25, 26
government of the Nez Perce, 16, 18, 26
heritage, 22
history, 4, 5, 6, 7, 8, 9, 10, 11, 12, 13, 14, 15, 22, 24, 25
homeland, 4, 12, 16, 26
horses, 10, 11, 22
Land Services Program, 26
language, 20, 21
Lewis and Clark expedition, 12
map, 4, 16, 23
members, 16, 18, 24, 26
name, 4, 5

National Chief Joseph Trail Ride, 22, 23
Nez Perce Friendship Feast, 23
Nez Perce Language Program, 20
Nez Perce tools, 9
reservation, 13, 14, 16, 17
Salmon River, 24
settlers, 14
timeline, 28–29
traditions, 4, 6, 7, 8, 9, 11, 20, 22, 23, 24, 26
treaty, 13, 26
U.S. Army, 14, 15, 22
U.S. government, 13, 26
warriors, 10, 14, 15

The images in this book are reproduced through the courtesy of: August Frank/ AP Images, cover; Joe Sohm, p. 3; Zack Frank, pp. 4-5; Imago History Collection/ Alamy, pp. 6, 28 (late 1600s to early 1700s); Everett Collection Historical/ Alamy, p. 7; Angel Wynn/ NativeStock, pp. 7 (baskets), 8 (fish trap), 23; Vasik Olga, p. 8; Thayne Tuason/ Wikipedia, p. 9 (hemp); AmBNPHOTO, p. 9 (corn husk); WBC ART/ Alamy, p. 9 (Nez Perce bag); Leon Werdinger/ Alamy, pp. 10-11; Makarova Viktoria, p. 11 (Appaloosa horse); Danita Delimont/ Alamy, p. 12; Gustav Sohon/ Washington State Historical Society, p. 13; DeLancey W. Gill/ Wikipedia, p. 14; unknown/ Wikipedia, pp. 15, 18 (flag); Witold Skrypczak/ Alamy, pp. 16-17; Stacia Morfin, p. 17; Bobjgalindo/ Wikipedia, p. 19 (Nimiipuu Health Center); © Deanpictures, p. 19; Lewiston Tribune/ AP Images, p. 20; Attasit Ketted, p. 20 (Nez Perce Language Program website); Kyle Mills/ AP Images, p. 21; NatPar Collection/ Alamy, p. 22; alacatr, pp. 24-25; Idaho Statesman/ Contributor/ Getty Images, p. 25; Susan Walsh/ AP Images, p. 26; Nature Picture Library/ Alamy, p. 27; Gustav Sohon/ Wikipedia, p. 28 (1855); Forest Service Northern Region/ Wikipedia, p. 29 (1986); Eric Isselee, p. 31.